Inclusive Hiring In Australia

Quick Guide For Employers

Matthew Levy OAM

Copyright © 2024 by Matthew Levy

All rights reserved.

No portion of this book may be reproduced in any form without written permission from the publisher or author, except as permitted by Australian copyright law.

This publication is designed to provide accurate and authoritative information in regard to the subject matter covered. It is sold with the understanding that neither the author nor the publisher is engaged in rendering legal, investment, accounting or other professional services. While the publisher and author have used their best efforts in preparing this book, they make no representations or warranties with respect to the accuracy or completeness of the contents of this book and specifically disclaim any implied warranties of merchantability or fitness for a particular purpose. No warranty may be created or extended by sales representatives or written sales materials. The advice and strategies contained herein may not be suitable for your situation. You should consult with a professional when appropriate. Neither the publisher nor the author shall be liable for any loss of profit or any other commercial damages, including but not limited to special, incidental, consequential, personal, or other damages.

Contents

About the author   1

Introduction   2

1. Introduction: Why Disability Inclusion Matters   3
2. Understanding Disability in the Workplace   6
3. Creating a Disability-Inclusive Hiring Strategy   9
4. Attracting Candidates with Disabilities   12

5. Accessible Recruitment and Interviewing Practices   15

6. Adapting the Workplace for Accessibility   18

7. Onboarding and Training for Inclusive Success   21

8. Supporting Career Development and Growth   24

9. Addressing Challenges and Overcoming Bias   27

10. Legal Requirements and Resources in Australia   30

11. Measuring and Sustaining Inclusion Efforts   33

12. Conclusion: Building a Future of Inclusive Employment   36

About the author

Matthew Levy has competed at five consecutive Paralympic Games, winning 3 gold, 1 silver, and 5 bronze medals. He's also swam at 5 World Swimming Championships - winning 20 international medals and holding 4 World Records. Matthew has a degree in Business (Management), an Australian Institute of Company Directors qualification and MBA (Leadership), as well as an Order of Australia Medal (OAM) for services to sport.

Introduction

This guide offers actionable strategies for hiring, supporting, and developing talent with disabilities, thus fostering diversity and innovation.

Chapter One

Introduction: Why Disability Inclusion Matters

Hiring people with disabilities goes beyond legal compliance – it's about building a diverse and innovative workforce. This chapter explains the positive impacts of inclusive employment, including enhanced creativity, morale, and corporate reputation. It also highlights statistics on disability employment in Australia and examples of companies worldwide leading in inclusivity.

- **Critical Insight**: Disability inclusion is not just an ethical responsibility; it's a strategic advantage. It can enhance problem-solving and boost innovation by bringing diverse perspectives to the table.

- **Awareness Point**: Inclusion isn't just a "nice-to-have"—research shows inclusive workplaces often see improvements in productivity and employee satisfaction.

My personal reflections

As a Paralympian, I've experienced how inclusive environments unlock potential. Disability inclusion is more than a concept; it's about giving everyone a fair shot to contribute. Competing alongside diverse teammates showed me that every individual brings unique strengths and inclusion fosters a culture of innovation and resilience.

Activity

Conduct a company-wide meeting to discuss the value of inclusivity. Share success stories and examples of companies benefiting from a diverse workforce.

Chapter Two

Understanding Disability in the Workplace

This chapter provides a comprehensive look at various types of disabilities – visible, invisible, physical, and intellectual – and explores common misconceptions. It emphasizes treating each employee as an individual, understanding unique needs, and using respectful language.

- **Critical Insight**: Disability can be visible or invisible, so sensitivity and awareness are essential. Employers must recognize that disabilities vary widely in form and may include physical, mental, and sensory impairments.

- **Awareness Point**: Be aware of the risks of stereotyping. Not all disabilities affect job performance in the same way, and adjustments may look different for each individual.

My personal reflections

In sports and beyond, disabilities vary widely – some are visible; others aren't. Competing alongside athletes with diverse challenges taught me the importance of understanding each person's unique needs and abilities. By breaking down stereotypes, we create spaces where everyone's talents are valued and respected.

Activity

Host a disability awareness workshop with experts who can provide insights on language, etiquette, and common workplace accommodations.

Chapter Three

Creating a Disability-Inclusive Hiring Strategy

Developing a strategic approach to inclusive hiring is essential. This chapter guides companies in creating a roadmap for disability inclusion. Topics include setting diversity goals, establishing clear policies, and identifying roles that could be adapted to attract a wider talent pool.

- **Critical Insight**: Developing a comprehensive hiring strategy involves setting goals, assessing job descriptions, and actively making roles accessible to people with disabilities.

- **Awareness Point**: Ensure policies don't inadvertently exclude candidates with disabilities by setting unnecessarily restrictive job criteria.

My personal reflections

Training as a Paralympian has taught me that preparation is key to success. When hiring, an inclusive strategy acts as the foundation of success. Just as athletes have different strengths, workplaces thrive when they create roles that recognise individual abilities and foster a truly diverse and adaptable workforce.

Activities

- Create a sample diversity and inclusion policy template.

- Facilitate a strategic planning session with leadership to outline inclusion goals, timelines, and measurable outcomes.

Chapter Four

Attracting Candidates with Disabilities

To attract candidates with disabilities, companies should look beyond traditional recruitment channels. This chapter covers outreach strategies such as partnering with disability employment services, engaging with community organisations, and creating inclusive job postings. It also emphasises using accessible and inclusive language.

- **Critical Insight**: Outreach matters. Employers are encouraged to partner with disability support organizations, which can bridge the gap between candidates and companies.

- **Awareness Point**: Job advertisements should be inclusive in language. Use terms that emphasize flexibility, accessibility, and openness to diverse abilities.

My personal reflections

In sports, visibility matters – seeing Paralympians compete inspires others to aim higher. Similarly, actively recruiting people with disabilities shows commitment to diversity. Partnering with organisations that support disabled talent brings in candidates who may not otherwise apply, as I've seen in both athletics and consulting.

Activity

Revise job postings using input from a disability employment service to ensure they are inclusive and inviting to candidates with disabilities.

Chapter Five

Accessible Recruitment and Interviewing Practices

This chapter provides actionable steps to create an accessible recruitment process. It covers accessible online applications, candidate accommodations, and bias-free interviewing techniques. Tips include using structured interview questions, offering alternate interview formats, and creating an inclusive interview environment.

- **Critical Insight**: Accessibility needs to start from the application process. Ensure online applications, assessments, and interviews accommodate various disabilities.

- **Awareness Point**: Offer options for reasonable adjustments without requiring candidates to disclose details about their disability upfront. This encourages a more comfortable and authentic interaction.

My personal reflections

As a Paralympian, I know that equitable opportunities are essential. Accessible recruitment allows candidates to showcase their abilities. Just as sports need adaptive equipment, interviews should accommodate diverse needs, giving all candidates a fair chance to excel and show how they could contribute to the team.

Activity

Train hiring managers on disability awareness and inclusive interviewing. For example, have them conduct mock interviews to practice accessibility-focused questions.

Chapter Six

Adapting the Workplace for Accessibility

Ensuring that the workplace is accessible is a key step in disability inclusion. This chapter offers guidance on physical and digital accessibility such as ramps, accessible desks, assistive technology, and workplace flexibility. It also includes steps for conducting an accessibility audit and implementing needed adaptations.

- **Critical Insight**: An accessible workplace can include physical adjustments (e.g., wheelchair ramps, ergonomic desks) and digital accommodations (e.g., screen readers, accessible websites).

- **Awareness Point**: Ensure both new and existing employees can easily request these modifications. Having clear processes in place shows a commitment to accessibility.

My personal reflections

In sports, accessibility is essential – whether it's adaptive equipment or modified training techniques. In the workplace, adaptations such as ergonomic desks and assistive technology ensure everyone can perform at their best. My Paralympic journey has shown me that these adaptations unlock potential and drive success.

Activities

- Have a checklist that includes accessibility features for physical spaces and helpful digital resources.

- Conduct a workplace accessibility audit that identifies areas for improvement and prioritises changes to create an inclusive environment.

Chapter Seven

Onboarding and Training for Inclusive Success

Onboarding sets the tone for an inclusive experience. This chapter discusses strategies to ensure onboarding is accessible, incorporate disability awareness training, and assign mentors. Tips on onboarding materials, introductions to resources, and creating a welcoming team culture are provided.

- **Critical Insight**: Effective onboarding sets the stage for a successful, inclusive experience. Providing tailored training programs and ensuring that accessibility needs are met early on is critical.

- **Awareness Point**: Avoid assuming that one-size-fits-all onboarding is effective. Ask employees what works best for them in terms of training and support.

My personal reflections

Paralympic teams prioritize inclusive onboarding, helping new members feel supported from day one. I've seen how mentorship and clear training in athletics empower members to thrive. In workplaces, similar strategies ensure that employees with disabilities feel welcome, valued, and set up for success.

Activity

Pair new hires with a buddy or mentor who can provide guidance and support to help ease the transition into the workplace.

Chapter Eight

Supporting Career Development and Growth

Career development opportunities empower employees with disabilities to grow and thrive. This chapter covers creating individualised development plans, offering mentorship, and providing skills training. Emphasis is placed on creating pathways to leadership for employees with disabilities.

- **Critical Insight**: Just hiring isn't enough—creating growth opportunities ensures long-term inclusion. Career progression, mentorship, and ongoing support are key elements.

- **Awareness Point**: Make sure that career development opportunities are communicated and accessible to all, and avoid unintentional bias in promotion criteria.

My personal reflections

Athletes are always pushing for personal growth. Throughout my journey, mentors and coaches helped me set and achieve goals. In business, offering development opportunities to people with disabilities builds their confidence and leads to employee retention, creating an environment where everyone can grow and contribute meaningfully.

Activity

Develop and launch a mentorship program for employees with disabilities that emphasises career growth and skills development.

Chapter Nine

Addressing Challenges and Overcoming Bias

Workplace bias can hinder inclusivity efforts. This chapter explores ways to identify and overcome biases through training, creating a culture of open communication, and setting up support systems to address disability-related concerns.

- **Critical Insight**: Bias can be a major barrier, even unintentionally. Training programs focused on unconscious bias help create a supportive environment where all employees can thrive.

- **Awareness Point**: Confront stereotypes directly. Equip team leaders and hiring managers to recognize and challenge their own biases.

My personal reflections

As a Paralympian, I've faced biases that overlook my capabilities. Open conversations and training can reduce these misconceptions, just as awareness-building has transformed perspectives in sports. Creating spaces for dialogue in the workplace helps break down stereotypes, fostering genuine inclusion.

Activity

Host an open forum on inclusivity, allowing employees to discuss challenges, share experiences, and provide feedback on workplace culture.

Chapter Ten

Legal Requirements and Resources in Australia

Compliance with legal requirements is essential. This chapter provides an overview of relevant Australian laws, including the Disability Discrimination Act 1992, and resources such as JobAccess, Disability Employment Services, and the Employment Assistance Fund, which provide support to both employers and employees.

- **Critical Insight**: Understanding legal obligations (e.g., Disability Discrimination Act) is essential to ensure fair and lawful treatment. Being aware of funding and resources available can help employers support their employees effectively.

- **Awareness Point**: Ignorance of these laws can lead to costly legal issues. Employers should stay informed about updates and changes in disability inclusion laws and standards.

My personal reflections

Understanding the support systems and legal protections in Australia helped me navigate my career as a Paralympian. In employment, resources such as JobAccess make a difference by ensuring organisations have the tools and knowledge to create an equitable, supportive environment for all.

Activity

Review the organisation's legal obligations and ensure the policies and practices align with Australian disability laws. Seek consultation if needed.

Chapter Eleven

Measuring and Sustaining Inclusion Efforts

Sustaining an inclusive culture requires ongoing assessment and adaptation. This chapter discusses ways to measure inclusion, such as employee feedback surveys, retention metrics, and progress tracking. Suggestions for adapting inclusion strategies over time are also included.

- **Critical Insight**: Metrics matter. Regularly assessing inclusion efforts helps in understanding what's working and what needs improvement.

- **Awareness Point**: Metrics should be meaningful; consider tracking retention rates, employee satisfaction, and productivity among employees with disabilities.

My personal reflections

In sports, progress is meticulously tracked, and the same should apply to inclusion. Regular feedback and tracking in the workplace ensure inclusion efforts remain effective. My experience has shown me that ongoing evaluation is key to creating an environment where everyone's needs are met and celebrated.

Activity

Set up a quarterly review of inclusion efforts by gathering feedback from employees with disabilities and tracking progress on inclusivity goals.

Chapter Twelve

Conclusion: Building a Future of Inclusive Employment

This final chapter encourages companies to view disability inclusion as an ongoing commitment. It summarises the key steps to creating a supportive, diverse workplace and emphasises the importance of leadership in driving long-term success.

- **Critical Insight**: Inclusion isn't a one-time effort; it requires ongoing commitment. Companies need to foster a culture where inclusivity is continually reinforced and expanded.

- **Awareness Point**: Inclusion requires all levels of the organization to participate actively, from leadership down to individual contributors. This chapter stresses the need for a continuous, long-term approach to creating a welcoming workplace for everyone.

My personal reflections

Inclusive employment is like building a great team – it requires continuous commitment. My time as a Paralympian taught me that inclusion isn't a one-time goal; it's a journey. By embracing diversity, workplaces can create a culture where everyone has a chance to succeed together.

Activity

Plan an annual event celebrating diversity and inclusion that recognises milestones and shares goals for the upcoming year.

Milton Keynes UK
Ingram Content Group UK Ltd.
UKHW020047271124
451585UK00012B/1113

9 781763 789531